Published in the United States of America
by Hallmark Cards, Inc.

ISBN: 0-87529-652-1

Library of Congress Catalog Number: 92-81183

Printed in the United States of America.

Now that you're 30, you may find it harder to get into:

A) This new music.

B) These new hairstyles.

C) Those narrow seats on airplanes.

What is This Object

1.) A circle symbolizing eternity.

2.) A button you've been meaning to sew on for about a year.

3.) The amount of patience you have for teenage salesclerks at discount stores.

Riddle!

Why does the 30-year-old wear red suspenders?

ANSWER: To keep his easy-fit, extra-room, elastic waistband casual pants up.

6.

How can the 30=year=old best make an enormous contribution?

A) By dedicating his life to others.

B) By working to achieve harmony in society.

C) By gathering up all those health and fitness magazines, all that exercise equipment, and all that attractive, trendy workout clothing, then donating them to his favorite charity so someone can actually use them.

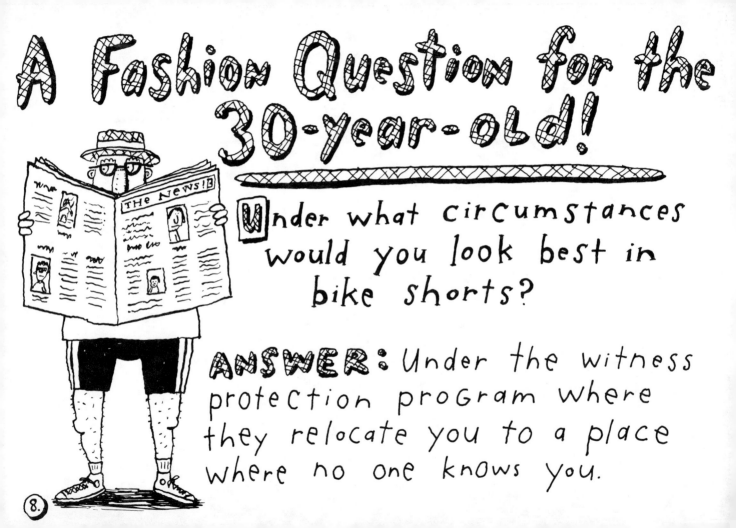

A Fashion Question for the 30-year-old!

Under what circumstances would you look best in bike shorts?

ANSWER: Under the witness protection program where they relocate you to a place where no one knows you.

Which is the 30-year-old's favorite kind of music?

A.) Anything with a thumping, pulsing beat.

B.) Anything sung by a group wearing spandex.

C.) Anything they made out to in high school or heard at a toga party in college.

True or False?

In some countries, 30 is considered the perfect age.

TRUE! But those countries also consider age spots and stretch marks signs of beauty.

10.

A Word Problem

IF a 30-year-old man leaves his home at 6 a.m. and drives east at 40 mph, and a 30-year-old woman leaves her home at 6:15 a.m. and drives west at 35 mph, when will they meet?

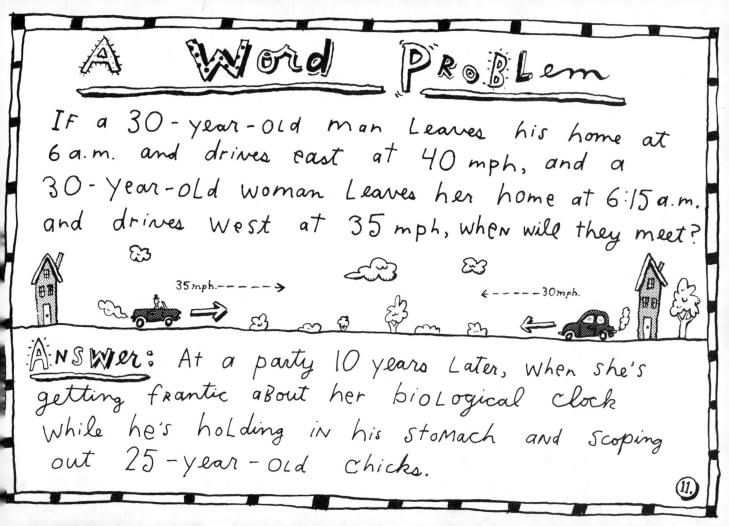

35 mph. - - - - →

← - - - - - 30 mph.

Answer: At a party 10 years later, when she's getting frantic about her biological clock while he's holding in his stomach and scoping out 25-year-old chicks.

11.

The three-word exclamation a 30-year-old is most likely to hear at the beach is:

A) "Hey sweet thing!"

B) "What a tan!"

C) "Thar she blows!"

How many words can you make from these letters?

THIRTY

ANSWER: Done for, finished, kaput, washed-up, wasted, pathetic, Life is over, old-timer.

13.

Most Socially-Conscious 30-year-Olds will readily Donate to:

 A.) PUBLIC TELEVISION.

 B.) PUBLIC RADIO.

 C.) PUBLIC FLOGGINGS OF ANYONE who LOOKS GOOD IN a SwimSuit.

TRUE OR FALSE?

There's still time for you to become famous and appear on television.

TRUE! Somebody could film you trying to blow out all those birthday candles, then send it to that funny home video program. ⑮

A 30-year old passes a mirrored wall in a mall. The first thought that comes to mind is:

A.) "Hey! I Look pretty Darn good!"

B.) "Not bad for 30!"

C.) "Wow... some people really let themselves go to he... Hey! That's me!"

Optical Illusion

Which diving platform is higher?

Answer: It doesn't matter. No way on Earth you'd go off either one at your age. Too risky.

18.

You know you're "30" because you've experienced a sudden urge to:

A. Go Windsailing.

B. Go Skydiving.

C. Go check your oil and buy more insurance.

TRUE OR FALSE?
Falling down a long, dark hole is a common 30-year-old's dream.
FALSE: 30-year-olds have by and large given up on their dreams.

What's wrong with this picture?

ANSWER: The convertible that the 30-year-old bought to feel young again isn't bright red.

A 30-year-old will often visit a specialist who offers:

A.) Aid in financial planning.

B.) Aid in choosing the right home.

C.) Aid in finding a knee brace that's attractive, yet functional.

SPECIALIST

A Brain-Teaser for the 30-Year-Old!

Why did you even get up today? You knew you were going to get mocked and picked on, didn't you? Why even get out of bed? Can you answer that one? Huh?

At 30, the sweet mystery of life is just beginning! No doubt you'll begin to find:

A.) Joy in unexpected places.

B.) Important life lessons in unexpected places.

C.) Gray hairs in unexpected places.

TRUE OR FALSE?

Most 30-year-olds are good in bed.

TRUE! They sleep later, snore louder and toss and turn more than just about anybody! ㉕

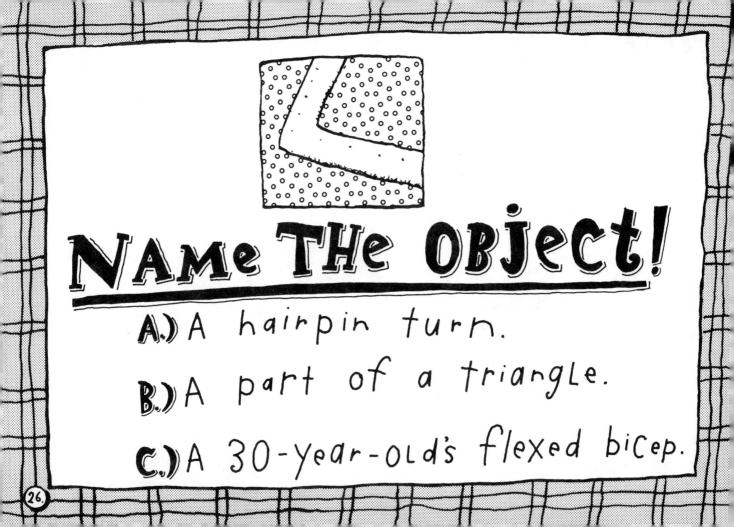

NAME THE OBJECT!

A.) A hairpin turn.

B.) A part of a triangle.

C.) A 30-year-old's flexed bicep.

Which of the following phrases is most likely to be uttered by a 30-year-old at a nightclub on a Friday night?

A.) "Diet cola, please."

B.) "I wish I could get my ferns to grow like this!"

C.) "Me? Uh... 27."

CONNECT THE DOTS to discover the average <u>number</u> of times the 30-year-old has sex in a month!

.1

.2

28.

When you step on an Elevator, you immedately think:

A.) What a great time-saver.

B.) Boy, my ankles would hurt if I had to climb all these stairs.

C.) Dig that crazy beat!

True or False?

Your formula for success at work is "Work hard and you'll go far!"

False! Your formula for success at work is Grecian.

30.

Riddle:

Why did the 30-year-old throw the clock out the window?

ANSWER: She thought it was a biological clock, and she was really tired of hearing it tick.

"Think GLOBALLY" is:

A.) A short, declarative sentence.

B.) A popular phrase used by environmentalists.

C.) A taunt yelled by passers-by as you enter a clothing store.

Q and A!

Q: IF the optimist sees the cup as half full, and the pessimist sees the cup as half empty, how does the 30-year-old see it?

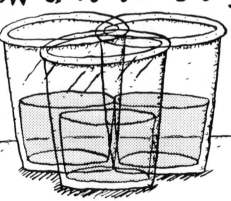

A: WiTH a nice pair of trendy wire-rim glasses.

1492 is:

A.) The year America was discovered.

B.) A great year for wine.

C.) Your age in Dog years.

Word Problem:

Two 21-year-olds, a 25-year-old and a 30-year-old are having fun at a late-night party. Suddenly, they run out of pizza. Whose job is it to go get more?

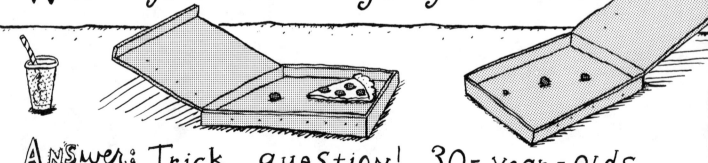

Answer: Trick question! 30-year-olds don't have fun at late-night parties!

Age 30 would be a good time to give up:

A.) Spicy Food.

B.) Staying out late.

C.) Yes, it would.

True or False?

Dashing hero ZORRO was actually 30.

False IF he was 30, he would have traded that "Z" he made with his sword for an "I." Less joint movement in the wrist.

38.

Which is the most appropriate gift to get a 30-year-old for his birthday?

A.) Money.

B.) A gift certificate.

C.) A book that mocks him.

TRUE OR FALSE?

Famous movie monster The Blob was actually 30.

FALSE If he'd been 30, he would have doubled in weight a lot faster.

"STORY" "PROBLEM"

A 30-year-old walked into a banker's office to sign his first mortgage loan. As he sat reading the papers that would commit him to endless years of payments, he thought about the awesome responsibility he was about to take on. He felt proud being able to cross that invisible line into true financial independence. The fleeting thought crossed his mind that once his father had done this same thing.

The theme of this story is:

A.) Being 30 can be an awesome responsibility.

B.) A 30-year-old can take pride in financial maturity.

C.) "Help! I'm turning into my Dad! Let me out of here!"

MORTGAGE

43.

WHat challenging sport is the 30-year-old most likely to engage in?

A.) Tennis.

B.) Basketball.

C.) Trying to fit into new jeans.

WHAT'S WRONG WITH THIS PICTURE?

ANSWER: It's an elevator at the office, and nobody has taped up a huge sign reading: "Guess Who's 30?"

WHICH OF THE FOLLOWING ARE YOU MOST LIKELY TO HEAR A 30-YEAR-OLD SAY IN A MOVIE THEATER?

A.) "The popcorn is great!"

B.) "The movie is interesting!"

C.) "My deck shoes are sticking to the floor!"

WORD PROBLEM

IF Betty's body is drooping at the rate of one inch per year, but she counteracts that with aerobics three times each week, what is her true droop rate?

Droopage = 1" per 365
subtract
AEROBICS
3 times
a week = 1
A yea

53
×3
156

365 ÷ 156
1   1

Answer: Trick question! Betty signed up for aerobics, but she never actually attends.

What is a 30-year-old most likely to order in a restaurant?

A.) A grilled bacon cheeseburger.

B.) Tofu salad.

C.) Whatever Hope and Michael would have ordered. She really misses them.

48.

True or False?

The 30-year-old defines "music videos" as "A relatively new medium incorporating the best of music and television."

False: A 30-YEAR-OLD DeFINES "music videos" as "A cHeap, inFerior SuBstitute for "American Bandstand."

49.

THE COLOR Red MAKES YOU THINK:
A.) Hot.
B.) SPORty.
C.) Stronger SPF.
NO TAN FOR THE BIG MAN
SPF-45

What is this?

A A baseball.

B A softball.

C The 30-year-old's stomach after a tummy tuck.

53.

Now that you're 30, you could best be described as:

A.) A party ANiMaL.

B.) A party Hearty kind of guy.

C.) A party of oNe.

Q and A

Q: In the event of an emergency like a tornado or a house fire, what does a 30-year-old immediately grab?

A: Her back! Any kind of tension makes it feel like she slept on a knotholed 2 by 4.

55

What do the following drawings represent?

A.

B.

A.) The pile of money you thought you'd have by now.

B.) The pile of money you actually have.

Choose the 30-year-old man's favorite magazine from the following list.

A.)
FORTUNE

B.)
GOLF DIGEST

C.)
TEENAGE AMAZON WOMEN WHO LUST AFTER OLDER GUYS

ANSWER: TRICK MAZE! There is no way out!

Hahahahahaha!!!

Just because you're 30, doesn't mean you have to:

A.) Slow down.

B.) Eat differently.

C.) Tell anyone.

True or False?

Popular fairy tale character Cinderella was 30.

False! If she'd been 30, the dancing would have made her feet swell and that glass slipper would have never come off.

Which is the scariest thought for the 30-year-old?

A.) The tensions and distrust between nations could lead to global war.

B.) Continued pollution of our environment will cause worldwide destruction.

C.) If I have a baby in the next 10 seconds, then when the baby is 17, I'll be 47, but if I wait another two or three years... I'll be 50!

PAT PAT

Name the OBJect!

A.) A golf tee that has been pushed in too far.

B.) An upside-down Christmas tree stand.

C.) A style of underwear you'll never own again.

IF the 30=year=old has yet to grow a decent mustache, it is probably best to:

A. Give up gracefully.

B. Try again when he's 40

C. Comb noseHair down and out.

64.

BRAIN TEASER!

IF a 30-year-old is jogging north on a two-mile track at 6 mph, and a 23-year-old is jogging south at 7mph, at what point will they pass?

ANSWER: Right in the spot where the 30-year-old has to stop and nurse his leg cramp.

What is the primary thought of a 30-year-old about to ride a merry-go-round?

A.) "What a classic piece of Americana!"

B.) "I love calliope music!"

C.) "This thing have a safety belt?"

THE AVERAGE 30-YEAR-OLD finds jogging and other movement-intensive exercises more painful to the joints as time goes on. The clever one combats this with:

A.) Plenty of deep-heating rub.

B.) Adequate stretching before and after.

C.) Pretty much constant whining to anyone with ears.

Karen, so this must be what hell is like.

I tell you Karen, my chiropractor is going to love this!

Karen? Karen?

In each of the following pairs of sports activities, only one is appropriate for the 30-year-old. Can you find it?

A.) Triathlon.

B.) Try-to-make-it-once-around-the-track-without-stopping-to-clutch-your-side-athlon.

A.) Snow Skiing.

B.) No Skiing.

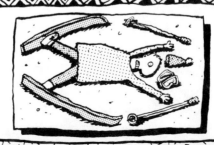

A.) Mountain Climbing.

B.) Molehill Climbing.

A.) Swimming the English Channel.

B.) Watching the Weather Channel.

A.) Pole-Vaulting.

B.) Poll Taking.

A.) Downhill Racing.

B.) Pretty much Downhill Everything.

Matching

Match the quote at the left with the famous 30-year-old at the right.

A.) "Let them eat cake. I'd better have the yogurt."

B.) "I cannot tell a lie... Except about my age."

C.) "I never met a burrito that liked me."

a.) George Washington

b.) Will Rogers

c.) Marie Antoinette

WRITTEN BY: Chris Brethwaite, Bill Bridgeman, Bill Gray, Allyson Jones, Kevin Kinzer, Mark Oatman, DeeAnn Stewart, Dan Taylor, Rich Warwick and Myra Zirkle.

Books from:

SHOEBOX GREETINGS

(A tiny little division of Hallmark)

STILL MARRIED AFTER ALL THESE YEARS
DON'T WORRY, BE CRABBY: Maxine's Guide to Life
40: THE YEAR OF NAPPING DANGEROUSLY
THE MOM DICTIONARY
THE DAD DICTIONARY
WORKIN' NOON TO FIVE: The Official Workplace Quiz Book
WHAT... ME, 30?
THE FISHING DICTIONARY
YOU EXPECT ME TO SWALLOW THAT? The Official Hospital Quiz Book
THE GOOD, THE PLAID AND THE BOGEY: A Glossary of Golfing Terms
THE CHINA PATTERN SYNDROME: Your Wedding and How to Survive It
THE GRANDPARENT DICTIONARY
STILL A BABE AFTER ALL THESE YEARS?
CRABBY ROAD: More Thoughts on Life From Maxine
THE HANDYMAN DICTIONARY A Guide For the Home Mess-It-Up-Yourselfer